D1605967

IF YOU WANT TO WALK ON WATER, YOU'VE GOT TO GET OUT OF YOUR BOAT

IF YOU WANT TO WALK ON WATER, YOU'VE GOT TO GET OUT OF YOUR BOAT

Walter Albritton

WORD BOOKS
PUBLISHER
4800 WEST WACO DRIVE
WACO, TEXAS
76703

IF YOU WANT TO WALK ON WATER, YOU'VE GOT TO GET
OUT OF YOUR BOAT!

Copyright © 1978 by Word, Incorporated
Waco, Texas 76703

ISBN 0-8499-0061-1

Library of Congress Catalog Card Number 77-88003

Printed in the United States of America

To Jamie . . .
Who came to me during the storm
and encouraged me to try
walking on water

Foreword by Maxie Dunnam

Introduction

Foreword

Walter Albritton is a contagious person. To be in his presence is to be drawn to him. To be drawn to him is to share in life at its fullest.

I like to laugh with Walter. He laughs with gusto. I like to pray with Walter. It is such an unself-conscious experience of communing with God—as natural as laughing. I like to share with him—to allow our souls to touch each other because he can feel with me and be with me in happiness and sorrow, in joy and pain.

And I'm glad to say I like to read Walter—because he writes the way he laughs, prays, and shares, in a warm, intimate, personal—yes, humorous, even light-hearted sort of way. Always, though simply stated, the message is profound and meaningful.

To read this book is almost as meaningful as being with Walter in person. That's the highest tribute I could pay. I can almost see his eyes light up as he tells of a boyhood experience of milking cows. I can almost see his eyes become misty as he shares about praying with a distressed mother over the telephone. I can almost feel the vibrations from his spirit as he shares his "impulsive" action—action prompted by the Holy Spirit. I can almost hear the excitement increase in his voice as he puts himself and leads us in imagination to put ourselves in Peter's sandals, get out of the boat in order to walk on the water.

This is a *good* book—good because it is easy to read, easy to understand, but more—good because it is helpful. It challenges, but it also offers practical directions for vibrant living as Christians. I almost said, "practical directions for walking on the water" but you may not be ready to believe that. After reading the book you will!

Maxie D. Dunnam
World Editor, *The Upper Room*

Introduction

While waiting for my druggist to fill a prescription, I noticed quite an assortment of massagers for sale. Among them were a shower massager, a back massager, and a foot massager. Jokingly I remarked that what I needed most was a massager for my mind! The druggist agreed.

Later it occurred to me that indeed we do have a mind massager, one fashioned by God himself—his sacred Word! Nothing is more mentally stimulating than earnest study of the Scriptures. And such study yields its greatest benefit when it involves more than the mere reading of words.

Over the centuries God's people have been encouraged to use all their senses in seeking the full meaning of the Scriptures. In our generation Lyman Coleman has introduced thousands of us to this wonderful mind-massaging method of Bible study with his *Serendipity* books, using an old idea in a fresh new way. Using our senses to really get into a scriptural scene can open up the corridors of our minds to fresh insight. And how the truth does stimulate!

I have experienced powerful massaging, awakening, and stroking of my spirit by using all my senses to get "into" one incident in the life of our Lord, and by trying to see, hear, feel, smell, and taste every aspect of the situation. No one scene has been more rewarding than the story told in the Gospels of Jesus and Peter walking on water. I have felt with Peter the solidity of the water for those few unbelievable steps, and I have felt with him the sudden fear as his feet began to sink beneath the surface.

I am convinced there is no way to predict the joy, the wonder, and the meaning that can come from intense, serious study of a single passage of the Scriptures. So I invite the thoughtful reader to come with me and get deeply "into" just twelve verses from the fourteenth chapter of Matthew.

In a real sense the journey of faith may be compared to walking on water. Faith always requires that we leave the boat of safety and risk following Christ into unknown waters frequented by storms. We grow and mature as his disciples only as we are willing to risk such faith every day throughout our lives.

In Alabama, walking on water is no strange phenomenon. We have often "seen" football Coach Paul "Bear" Bryant of the University of Alabama walk on water!

So come with me and let us try what Peter tried. Just remember one thing: if you want to walk on water, you've got to get out of your boat!

As Jesus said to Peter, "Come on!"

WALTER ALBRITTON

Demopolis, Alabama

IF YOU
WANT TO
WALK ON WATER,
YOU'VE GOT TO
GET OUT OF
YOUR BOAT

1

A Time to Pray

Directly after this, Jesus insisted on his disciples' getting aboard their boat and going on ahead to the other side, while he himself sent the crowds home. And when he had sent them away he went up the hillside quite alone, to pray. When it grew late he was there by himself. . . . *Matthew 14:22, 23*

It is not unusual to read in the Gospels that Jesus went aside to pray. A quiet time seems to have been one of his habits. Jesus knew the energizing power of God–centered solitude. He was given strength during moments alone with God that sustained him during the pressure of his demanding ministry with people.

Jesus did not always choose the same time for solitude. When needs arose which demanded the power he found in prayer, he went aside to get it. A familiar chorus speaks of "Jesus in the morning, Jesus at the noon time, and Jesus when the sun goes down." It seems clear that Jesus often enjoyed a quiet time at each of these time periods, and at other times whenever he felt there was a need for it.

His reasons for solitary prayer are more important than the time of the day he chose. John Wesley habitually rose to pray at four o'clock each morning. His decision to do so was inspired partly by the example of Jesus in Mark 1:35—"Then, in the early morning, while it was still dark, Jesus got up, left the house and went off to a deserted place, and there he prayed."

In the story we are considering here in Matthew 14, the occasion of Jesus' solitude was late evening. Earlier in the same chapter Jesus chose to be alone during the day, as soon as he received the tragic news that John the Baptist had been beheaded. "When he heard it he went away by boat to a deserted place, quite alone" (Matt. 14:13).

Jesus encountered many needs which he felt he could not handle without God–focused solitude. Observe at least these examples with me:

When he was distressed. Learning that his friend John had been beheaded, Jesus was troubled and went immediately to be alone with his Father. If he was not momentarily fearful that his own ministry might be terminated prematurely, he was at least saddened by the cruel fate of a good man of God. This was the man who had baptized him in the river Jordan, who had sought to prepare the people to receive the message Jesus was preaching.

The medicine God gave Jesus during solitude worked well, for he soon returned to his work, speaking the good news of the kingdom, and feeding the hungry five thousand. If our Lord Jesus needed this medicine, do we not need it all the more? Will it not heal us as well of our distress and enable us to return with enthusiasm to joy and usefulness in daily living?

When he was weary. Jesus experienced the very human feeling of becoming tired. As he ministered to people, touching them and healing them, power went "out of him." His strength left him. So he went aside to pray that he might be renewed, replenished with spiritual power.

Constant contact with people wearies the best of us, especially when we are caring and giving to others as Jesus was. All work and no prayer makes the Christian a dull—and exhausted—person! Understanding this, Jesus followed God's rhythmic plan— exhaling and inhaling, activity and rest, service and solitude. Can you and I afford to do any less than accommodate ourselves to this plan which is so plainly visible in the very nature of life all around us?

When he wanted his perspective corrected. John tells us that after Jesus had fed the five thousand, many of the people became so excited that they wanted to make him their king. When Jesus realized their intentions, "he retired once more to the hillside quite alone" (John 6:15).

The fiery temptations Jesus faced in the wilderness were not the last he battled. Remember how Luke described the conclusion of the wilderness experience: "And when the devil had exhausted every kind of temptation, he withdrew until his next opportunity" (Luke 4:13).

First the devil had tried to give Jesus a kingdom, and now the people were tempting him with such an offer. Jesus knew his Father had not sent him into the world to make him a king. But such talk would be tempting to any man. So when he was faced with a possible confusion of his values, Jesus retreated to a quiet place where his mind might be cleared and his perspective corrected as he talked with his Father.

How much of our confusion might be cleared if we habitually checked out the advice of men in quiet conversation with our heavenly Father? If Jesus needed such mind–clearing time, do we not need it more?

When he wanted guidance for important decisions. Though Jesus was the Son of God, he did not automatically know the will of God. He had to seek it, and at least on one occasion he found it necessary to extend his quiet time through a whole night. Evidently he wanted confirmation from his Father concerning his choice of apostles, so he spent valuable time meditating on the names of the twelve. Luke tells us "that he went up the hillside to pray, and spent the whole night in prayer to God. When daylight came, he summoned his disciples to him and out of them he chose twelve whom he called apostles" (6:12, 13).

We may be sure that there were many other occasions when Jesus went aside to ask for direction. Perhaps it was because he found his Father so willing to give guidance that he taught his disciples simply to ask and expect to receive a ready answer from a loving God.

His earthly ministry was brief, but many important decisions faced Jesus during his short years. Consumed with a desire to do the will of God, he sought daily guidance so that he might not choose the wrong road. It was not easy for him, and it is never easy for any man, no matter how committed, to be certain his decisions are within God's will. After spending time alone with his Father, Jesus never hesitated. In quietness came confidence so that he moved with assurance; "he resolved to go to Jerusalem" (Luke 9:51).

Think of the heartache we have brought upon ourselves because we took no time to pray before making big decisions! Think, too, of the joy we may know when we take the time to receive guidance from God so that the right decision is made about a job, a marriage partner, a moral question, a college, a business partner, a home. Surely if Jesus could discover God's will in solitude, we can, too!

When he found it difficult to do the will of God. In the garden of Gethsemane on the Mount of Olives, Jesus went to his "usual place," his disciples with him. "Then he went off by himself, about a stone's throw away, and falling on his knees, prayed in these words—'Father, if you are willing, take this cup away from me—but it is not my will, but yours, that must be done'" (Luke 22:39-42).

Here again Jesus is alone with God, this time struggling with the guidance he has received. He knows what his Father's will is, but he would rather not do it if there is any other way out. How common an experience that is! Notice what Jesus does not do, as well as what he does do. He does not seek the advice of the twelve. Rather, in solitude again he talks— and listens—to his Father! The struggle is real. So intensely does he pray that his sweat becomes like great drops of blood. Finally, the matter is resolved with Jesus submitting to his Father's will, even if it is hard. Nothing matters more to him than his obedience.

Apparently, an attitude of submission did not come easily to Jesus. But once he made that surrender, observe the response of God: the strengthening angel attended Jesus immediately! God respects the free will he has given his children, but once they choose his will, they are never left alone! Jesus was not left alone, and neither are we.

Some men do not seem much concerned about the will of God. They simply do "what they think is best," floating along on choices which are grounded in their own selfishness. If they ever give much thought to the will of God, it is with the attitude that God is surely a nice fellow and he will understand. Eventually everything will work out for the best. We see none of this blasé attitude in the example of our Lord.

If we follow in his steps, we too will discover it is not always easy to do the will of God. We may struggle for an understanding of what he wants—and then wish we hadn't found it! But if we are willing to find that solitary garden, to surrender our wills, trusting that his way is best, we may joyfully discover that the strengthening angel has come to us also! Fanny Crosby must have often wished for sight instead of blindness, yet in a beautiful surrender akin to that of Jesus she could cling to the Father's will in childlike trust:

> All the way my Savior leads me—
>   What have I to ask beside?
> Can I doubt His tender mercy,
>   Who through life has been my Guide?
> Heavenly peace, divinest comfort,
>   Here by faith in Him to dwell!
> For I know, whate'er befall me,
>   Jesus doeth all things well.

When he prayed for his friends. Peter had many unique experiences with Jesus. One in particular stirs my heart as I think what it must have been like to have been in Peter's shoes. Put yourself in this scene and get "inside" Peter's skin as you read Luke's description:

> Oh, Simon, Simon, do you know that Satan has asked to have you all to sift like wheat?—But I have prayed for *you* that you may not lose your faith. Yes, when you have turned back to me, you must strengthen these brothers of yours (22:31, 32).

How would you feel, having Jesus look into *your* eyes and say, "I have prayed for *you* that you may not lose your faith"? What would you say in reply? Imagine what a soul–stirring moment that must have been for Peter—to discover that the Savior of the world has been on his knees lifting you up to the Father!

Peter evidently was so impressed that he forgot what he was saying, for he quickly made a promise he was not strong enough to keep! Jesus knew he was weak—so weak that he would soon deny his Savior three times! Yet, knowing this, Jesus still believed in Peter. He could pray without resentment that strength would come to his impetuous friend!

What would it mean to you, to have such a friend? One who believed in you even when you were about to fall on your face in disgrace? One who would not give up on you but would continue to lift you up in prayer, believing that eventually you would turn out all right? Would that not cause hope to remain alive in your heart?

Or look at this matter from another point of view.

Think of your friends, your close friends. See their faces. Imagine what it would mean to anyone of them if you could have the attitude toward each one that Jesus showed toward Peter. What a difference it would make if even one of your friends saw in your eyes a love that simply would never give up on him!

Jesus went aside to pray for his friends, but he never boasted of such praying, nor did he speak of praying for another as though he were superior. We may be sure that as he prayed for Peter he also prayed for Judas, Thomas, Andrew, and the other disciples. But, so far as we know, he did not tell them, though they surely knew it. This can serve as a cue for us. Only on rare occasions does it seem wise to tell our friends we are praying for them. His Spirit can guide us in knowing when it is appropriate.

We have no option! We *must* pray for our friends as they face the demands and pressures, the heartaches and sorrows of daily living. Can we do less than follow the example of our Lord? Can we, for that matter, do better?

In *The Robe*, by Lloyd C. Douglas, Justus tries to convince Marcellus, the Roman centurion, that Jesus is alive. Marcellus is very skeptical, but Justus persists, saying that sometimes "I feel aware of him, as if he were close by." Marcellus replies that he would feel very uncomfortable if he were being perpetually watched by some invisible presence.

Justus responds with a beautiful insight, "Not if that presence helped you defend yourself against yourself, Marcellus. It is a great satisfaction to have someone standing by—to keep you at your best."

As we make the Christian journey, we, too, experience the joy of his presence standing by. And beyond that, we can become to our friends a visible presence, a loving, caring friend standing by to help another do his best. But such Christian friendship is not likely to happen unless it is grounded in loving prayer offered to God in a lonely place.

Now take inventory of your reasons for a quiet time. We have observed some of the needs which caused Jesus to go aside. You can think of others which motivate you. Go back and underline those above which apply to you. Name two or three others as you think about your own prayer life:

_____

_____

_____

Think back over your life and try to estimate how many hours you have spent in quiet meditation and prayer alone with God. Would they add up to several days? Several weeks? Several months? Looking at it in comparison with hours spent in other activities will help you decide how important prayer is to you. Make a graph below showing how a week of your time is spent. Include such activities as Bible–reading, eating, working, sleeping, and solitary praying.

If you are like most of us, you find it difficult to set aside time for quiet prayer. What barriers can you think of personally (such as "never enough time," "hard to get up early")? List your barriers:

_____

_____

_____

Now take your pen and cross out any of your barriers which you feel are more "excuses" than real reasons for not spending time in prayer. Then look ahead. Suppose you live ten more years. How many hours in those ten years would you like to devote to a quiet time? _____ You realize, of course, that the best way to make prayer a priority is to make time for it daily. Think about your daily routine: what hour of the day would be good to use as your quiet time if one is not already a habit with you?

_____

Promise yourself you will begin today! And if you fail to continue your routine faithfully, start over again! Remember that it was for people like you, and Peter, and me that Jesus was willing to keep on believing in until they got it all together!

Most of us encounter many obstacles in making the best use of our quiet time. Distractions often cause us to waste time even when we are disciplined enough to go aside daily. So we need to explore new ways of making "contact" with his presence, and appropriating all the blessings from solitude that God is prepared to give us.

I have found the method of St. Sulpice, a French priest of the seventh century, most helpful in improving the results of my devotional life in the Word. His plan for meditation involves three steps: Jesus before the eyes, Jesus in the heart, and Jesus in the hands. In the first step, you observe, using all your senses to increase your awareness of the subject being considered. If it is the scene of the woman touching the hem of Jesus' garment, for instance, you would use all the senses to gain a total awareness of the situation.

In step two, Jesus in the heart, you join the scene and participate in it. You might take the role of the woman, trying to imagine how you would react when finally you are face to face with Jesus.

Jesus in the hands, step three, calls for decision and action based on what you have observed and participated in. What will you do about what you have experienced? Hear Jesus saying to you alone, "And now, what will *you* do?" Such meditation is best concluded in an attitude of thanksgiving, thanking the Lord for providing strength and grace to carry out the resolutions that must be acted upon.

Experiment with this Sulpician Method in your next quiet time. You might select Acts 16:16–34 as your scene and subject for meditation. See yourself as the jailor. Really try to get "inside" the man, and use all your senses to become aware of what he experienced. Try to "feel" his fear, his amazement, his gratitude, his joy. Then invite the Holy Spirit to open up for you what you must do in light of what you have seen and heard. Thank him for giving you the grace to act on your plans.

Perhaps Jesus often took time to pray because there is so much to learn! And it may happen to us, as it did to our Lord, that spending quality time in God–focused solitude will enable us to become caught up entirely in the will and service of God!

2

A Time to See

When it grew late he was there by himself, while
the boat was by now a long way from the shore at
the mercy of the waves, for the wind was dead
against them. *Matthew 14:24*

While Jesus was in prayer, his disciples were in
trouble. They had obeyed Jesus, trying to cross the
lake as he had instructed them. But sudden storms
on the sea of Galilee were common, and the disciples
found themselves in quite a struggle with the wind
and the waves. Their obedience had not necessarily
kept them out of trouble. Even so, it rarely does with
any of us.

People who want to bargain with God can learn a
great lesson from the plight of the disciples. Some
folks say to God, "I'll obey you if you will save me
from pain and trouble." Theirs is a "fair weather"
religion. At the first serious difficulty they encounter,
they discard all pretense of faith. But God does not
promise us clear sailing on a smooth sea. His promise
is simply that He will be with us no matter what we
have to face.

Even with this understanding, however, it is often
hard for us to believe, really believe, that God is
aware of our situation, that the Creator of the uni-

verse really cares. We tend to fall into the pagan concept of God: that he has neither time for us nor personal interest in us, and that we have to yell and pound on the door of heaven to get his attention. As faith gives way to doubt, each of us is apt to think, *I am just one insignificant person among four billion people, so God could not possibly be aware of me.*

That is why it is so important for us to understand the biblical witness about the nature of God. God was "in Christ," Paul said, so when we look at Jesus we are looking into the face of almighty God. In the words of Jesus, "The man who has seen me has seen the Father" (John 14:9). If, then, Jesus was aware of the trouble of people, if he actually cared, then we have evidence that God cares!

Now back to the disciples in the storm: Is Jesus aware of their distress? Yes! While Matthew merely implies that Jesus sees his friends in trouble, Mark makes it clear with the beautiful expression: "He *saw* them . . ." (6:48). So Jesus was not so absorbed in prayer that he failed to see the misfortune of others. What a marvelous insight into the nature of God!

As I was writing this, I was interrupted by a telephone call from a distressed mother. Her little girl has been sick with fever for weeks, and the doctor has been unable to pinpoint the problem. Out of her anguish she called to ask me to pray for her daughter. I asked her to let me pray over the phone. In my prayer I said, "Lord, we know that you care about this little girl because in the Gospels we see Jesus loving little children, taking them up in his arms and blessing them. So we ask you to bless this mother's child and heal her of this illness."

How thrilled I was to be able to believe that God really does care about this mother and her child! Those few moments were alive with the presence of God! It gave meaning to my life to have another person share her burden with me. I feel grateful to God that he enabled me to be aware of her need, to feel her suffering in my own heart as I remembered the illnesses of my own children. I shudder to think that I might have missed this opportunity to be a sensitive, caring person by simply being "too busy" to receive telephone calls!

In Acts we see Peter and John on their way to the temple for a prayer meeting. They had prayer on their minds. But fortunately they *saw* the lame man at the gate. When the man spoke to them, Luke says that "Peter *looked* intently at the man and so did John" (Acts 3:4). They had to "see" him before they could become aware of his need and be in a position to help him. Before Pentecost, Peter had not been too observant of the needs of others; he had himself on his mind constantly! Now, empowered by the resurrected Christ, he had "eyes" to see people in a way he had never seen them before. With new life in Christ had come new vision.

A friend of mine says that Christ has affected her sight in an interesting way. For years she could not look directly at people. She was shy, withdrawn, insecure, with very low self–esteem. As she grew in faith, Christ slowly helped her to accept herself as a person of worth. Gradually she began to be able to look into the eyes of other people. Accepting her own acceptance by God, she was able to accept others. Once Christ helped her to look at herself, she was able to look at others.

To live in Christ is to live with an understanding sensitivity to the people around us. And it takes a lifetime of growing really to become aware of others. We are apt to get so wrapped up in ourselves that we look "past" people, seeing only human forms and failing to see real persons with crushed dreams, broken hearts, and feelings like our own.

Imagine for a few minutes the situation Jesus was in on the lonely hillside. It was quiet and peaceful there. He had been through a tiring day. Now he was being renewed as he enjoyed communion with God. Seeing the disciples in trouble on the lake was an interruption of a beautiful quiet time. Perhaps he might have thought, *That storm is not a bad one; it will blow over soon. Surely they won't need me. They can handle the boat themselves.*

Is this not the way we ourselves often rationalize when the distress of others is before our eyes? "They can get along without us. After all, every man must look out for himself!"

Take a few minutes now to close your eyes and think about your own friends, the people you work with, your neighbors, your family, the people you see daily. Let their faces roll across the screen of your mind as you think over an ordinary day. Do you really "see" these people? Are you genuinely aware of them as persons? Of all these persons, is there one who perhaps has wanted to share with you his personal distress but has never felt that you had time or cared? Try to imagine a conversation with this person after he discovers that you really "see" him as a person.

It is a great thing to know that another person is

really aware of you, trying to understand you and communicate with you. On the other hand, it is extremely frustrating to be with someone who is obviously preoccupied, thinking of something else, looking down rather than into your eyes. Such an individual gives the impression that he is bored and that you are a person he finds uninteresting.

I have caught myself on many occasions "drifting away" from someone who has stopped by the office to chat. One man recently had been with me only a few minutes when I realized I was not really listening to him. I didn't really "see" him. I saw what I wanted to be doing. Something else was more important than this man. He must have sensed my lack of awareness, for he picked up his hat as though he were about to leave. Immediately I "saw" him! The Holy Spirit opened my eyes, curing me of my momentary blindness. As I gave myself to my friend in sensitive awareness, he relaxed and shared with me for more than thirty minutes. We "saw" each other and were blessed by the communion of loving awareness.

Get a picture of Jesus coming to you. You are distressed over your blindness, your lack of awareness of others. You ask Jesus to heal you. He reaches out; and as he does you see his eyes. In his eyes you see great compassion as he gazes intently into your eyes. It is as though he sees into your very soul! Then he touches you and your sight is restored. And you hear him gently say, "Go, and do not fail to see your brothers in their need, for in seeing them, you will see me also."

"He who hath eyes to see, let him see!"

3

A Time to Go

In the small hours Jesus went out to them, walking on the water of the lake. *Matthew 14:25*

The authentic Christian will learn to spend time in prayer, alone with God. He will develop a sensitive awareness to the needs of people around him. But he must not stop short of a third essential quality —a willingness to *go* to those whose needs are in focus before him.

In Jesus we see a balance of praying with going. He went apart to pray. He was not so preoccupied with kingdom business that he failed to be aware of the plight of people near him. And seeing men in distress, he went to them. He made himself and his resources available.

Some people seem to be good at meditation; they are skillful in spinning ideas. They may even be keen enough to observe the circumstances of others around them. But what good is the best philosophy if it does not issue in action that benefits people? Jesus could think. He could pray. He could speak with power. "No man ever spake like that!" (John 7:46). But he knew when it was time to go! So he went to the rescue of his disciples.

Love made him go. Love always makes going

necessary. Because he loved his disciples, he could not stand idly by and see them overcome by the storm. It is the very nature of love that we make ourselves available to those we care about.

To be available is to be accessible, obtainable. This was the pattern of Jesus' ministry. When the disciples thought him too busy to be bothered with little children, he insisted on being available. Remember how Luke described the scene:

> The people began to bring babies to him so that he could put his hands on them. But when the disciples noticed it, they frowned on them. But Jesus called them to him, and said: "You must let little children come to me, and you must never prevent their coming. The kingdom of Heaven belongs to little children like these" (18:15, 16).

Again when the "woman who had had a hemorrhage for twelve years" touched Jesus in the crowded street, Peter felt that Jesus had no time to be bothered (Matt. 9:20). After all Jesus was already on a mission of mercy, going to the home of Jairus, whose daughter was dying. How beautiful that Jesus had time for this poor woman, that he was sensitive to her situation, that he was accessible in her hour of need! If Jesus had a habit of praying, he also had a habit of being available to people!

And over the centuries the living Christ has continued this practice of becoming available to believers. During the writing of this book, I was awakened one night from a deep sleep. As I sat up in bed I had a mental image of Jesus standing before me with his right arm uplifted. Though I heard no audible sound, I knew Jesus was speaking these words to me: "Go on, for I am with you!" I looked at my watch and was amazed to see that it was 3 A.M.—the very hour Matthew says it was when Jesus walked over the water to the disciples! As I lay back down to think and eventually go back to sleep, I knew that the words of Jesus had to do with this book, for I had been doubtful about ever completing it. He had seen me in my distress and had come to me, even me!

Our journey as Christians is one of coming and going: Christ coming to us and enabling us in our going to others. He comes to us to cleanse, renew, encourage, equip. Then he sends us out to others daily, sharing his love, helping us to pay the costly price of being available to others.

When a friend of ours was dying with cancer, my wife Dean caught a plane and went to his bedside in the hospital. Though she could not rescue him from the storm of cancer, she had to go. Love insisted on her going. Conversation was difficult, and her words seemed futile. After a while she decided that she might relieve some of his discomfort by rubbing his feet. The rubbing was helpful physically, and emotionally also. With tears rolling down both cheeks, our friend spoke words which are forever etched in Dean's mind: "You know," he said, "I am fifty-two years old, and this is the first time anyone has ever rubbed my feet." Dean knew that our Lord had met the two of them there in a sacred moment made possible because one person had made herself available to another in need.

A father and mother faced a difficult hour in court. Their son was brought before the judge on a drug charge. During the tense moments of waiting, a friend slipped in beside them, somehow to share the anxiety. This friend had prayed. She knew the need. But praying and knowing were not enough—going was added. Her presence added strength and encouragement to those nervous parents. Whatever the judge's decision, the decision of the friend to come to them would be long remembered.

I wish you could know my friend Paul Molyneux, who is a retired druggist almost ninety years old. Paul helped people during his years as a druggist, but since his retirement he has had a marvelous ministry of helpfulness. Assisting a nursing home with its needs for medicine, he became aware of the patients. Many he had known in earlier years, and many he soon discovered were lonely and discarded by their families. So for years Paul has gone to these patients, cheering them up with his friendly spirit, bringing them magazines, chatting about old times, wheeling some who cannot walk outside for some sunshine, caring about them as though they were members of his own family. Such going Jesus apparently has honored, for the going and caring seem to have added years as well as joy to an old man. Paul's own wife died years ago. He could have "holed up" in his little house and spent his remaining years watching television and remembering the good old days. But he did not. There is in his heart this desire to be a disciple of Jesus, so he goes about reaching out to others with hands of love. It is as though he himself were guided by an unseen hand. Perhaps that is exactly what is happening. It is the only way you can explain such a man!

I turned to Francis Schaeffer's book, *The Church at the End of the Twentieth Century,* hoping to discover something unusual and exciting for the years ahead. I had to laugh as I found Schaeffer talking, not about something new and different, but about the need of the church to practice "costly, observable love"! His emphasis is on love that is visible, that demonstrates its reality in ways observable to bystanders.

Such love is made visible only by available disciples, whose going is made possible by the Christ who keeps coming to them!

Close your eyes and listen carefully. You may hear the turbulent winds of personal storms in which some of your closest friends are struggling to survive. Is there not at least one who might be "saved" by your love, if you took the time to go to him? And is that not the kind of observable love which you and I must practice today, even before the end of the twentieth century?

Jesus went to them. Go thou and do likewise!

4

The Fear We All Feel

When the disciples caught sight of him walking on the water they were terrified. "It's a ghost!" they said, and screamed with fear. Matthew 14:26

Most of us can identify with the little boy who was afraid to go outside his home at night. He was simply afraid of the dark. When his mother insisted, he held back, saying, "But something might get me."

Trying to reassure him, his mother replied, "Go on out and play, son. You'll be all right. God is out there and he'll take care of you."

His courage built up, the boy stuck his head out the door, peering intently into the darkness. Finally he stepped outside a few feet, stopped, and spoke out boldly: "Okay, God, if you're out there, don't move a muscle or you'll scare me to death!"

I could have been that boy. As a lad I was always uneasy in the dark. I could walk about on our farm quite unafraid during the daylight hours. But let the shadows fall and I saw and heard awful monsters everywhere!

The barn was about 100 yards from our house, and in the winter months, when the days were short, I often had to finish milking the cows in the dark. A flashlight usually provided what light I had. No one ever clocked me, but I am positive I established a record as the world's fastest milker in those days. And sometimes I raced so hard through the darkness to the house that I arrived with less milk in the bucket than when I left the barn!

It has been fun to walk back over some of those childhood steps and recall my fear, realizing now that the monsters I feared then never really existed, except in my imagination. Yet the fear was real, and sometimes even now the darkness of unfamiliar places can trigger a sudden flush of fear. It was real then, and it is real now, even though I know there are no strange, menacing creatures behind every tree.

Fear is real for us all. It is a normal human emotion, though its causes may vary. Even though we cannot eliminate it from our lives, we can learn to handle it. Actually, our capacity to be fearful is a blessing in many ways. Fear of being killed in a highway accident may cause us to drive more carefully and thus save our lives. Fear of electricity saves the lives of electricians every day! Fear of drowning causes the swimmer to observe rules that insure his safety.

But fear can get out of hand and become quite harmful; it can make us miserable and take the fun out of living. Unless we find a way to hold fear in check, it can destroy us. And it seems to be always lurking in the dark places of our lives, seeking a way to take control of us. It can take hold in a small, insignificant circumstance and begin to snowball.

As I prepared to make a long journey, flying from the Gulf Coast in Mobile, Alabama, to the Bering Sea coast in Nome, Alaska, I had an unexpected battle with snowballing fear. I had not given much thought to the danger of flying 10,000 miles until one of my friends remarked, on the Sunday before my departure, "It really seems foolish for you to make this trip. You have a wife and four sons here in Mobile, and you could be killed trying to fly to Alaska. After all, your family needs you far more than those people in Alaska do!"

It was not easy to dismiss her remark. Was this a warning from God not to go? I thought not, so decided to go ahead with my plans. On the morning of my departure my wife and two of the boys drove me to the airport. On the way we decided to stop for a cup of coffee. As we were getting out of the car, Steve broke the silence with a remark that was quite solemn, no sign of humor at all: "Well, one last cup of coffee with my daddy!"

His words stunned me so I couldn't comment, and no one else said anything either. My wife said later she didn't even remember Steve saying that, but I surely did! His words rang in my ears all the way to Nome!

In fact, I began to wonder before we landed in Nome if Steve had not been a prophet. As we approached Nome, the pilot advised us to prepare for landing. We were aware that it was snowing below, for every other flight to Nome that day had been canceled. Peering out the window, I could see nothing but a solid mass of white. The pilot dropped lower and lower, searching for the runway. Then just as we thought he might touch down, he revved those powerful jet engines and climbed back above the snow.

Four times he tried to land, and four times he

changed his mind! All the time I was fighting fear that kept saying, "They were right. This is the end. You're soon to be killed. You should have stayed at home!" I might have been overcome by fear except for one thing: I remembered that I am a Christian! I remembered that I was not alone, that Christ was with me! A stabilizing peace seemed to fill me, and I began to pray a simple prayer over and over: "Lord, as you made a way for Moses through the wilderness, please make a way for us through this snow!"

In a few minutes we landed safely, and I stepped out on cold ground, minus the cold fear that had threatened to envelop me. During the next few days God blessed my preaching and confirmed through many glowing faces that it was indeed his will for me to make that long journey! I was so filled with gratitude all the way home that fear could find no opening to come back inside me.

Matthew could give a vivid report that the disciples screamed with fear, because he was right there with them. As he wrote his Gospel, he remembered well the fear they all felt as they saw Jesus approaching them, walking on the water. They were already anxious because of the storm; the sight of a man, even Jesus, walking on water only intensified their fear.

To be a man is to experience fear. And fear has many faces. At times fear may wear the face of danger. Or it may wear the face of insignificance; a man may fear that his life is adding up to nothing more than a big fat zero. Winston Churchill was voted the most influential man of the twentieth century, but his son Randolph said, "I constantly had to reas-

sure my father that his life had not been a failure."
Churchill feared meaninglessness, as do most men at
one time or another. We want to know that we count!
We want to believe that life makes sense and that
our efforts make a difference.

Fear may come barging in, wearing the face of
failure. We want to succeed, but we fear that we may
not. Often it is the fear of failing that causes us to
fail. So fear defeats us. As a man I discovered that I
had nursed a fear from childhood that I could never
do anything right. Whatever I attempted, there was
always the nagging fear that someone else could have
done it better, and my efforts would fall just short of
the mark. Even when others called my work a success, I was still doubtful, unable to accept a success-
ful me as the real me.

As a youth I was awkward in using a hammer and
a saw. My father tried to pass his own skill on to me,
but often he would take the hammer from me impa-
tiently, saying, "If that is the best you can do, give
me the hammer!"

As a preacher years later I sometimes struggle with
this fear that keeps hanging on. It is almost as though
I fear God will step out from behind some curtain
and say, "If that is the best you can do, give me that
Bible!" But when this fear rears its ugly head, I remember that I am a Christian. Because I belong to
Christ, I can handle fear. I can succeed. and I can
fail. But I am still His, and He is mine.

And there is no resentment toward my father for
having snatched the hammer from my hands. He was
doing the best he could. Sometimes as a father he
failed; sometimes he succeeded. I have to laugh,

too, rather than fret about my father's mistakes; for now I am the father, with four sons who are awkward in using hammers, and I am the impatient father saying, "Give me that hammer!" What comfort there is in knowing that if God could help me become a responsible man in spite of my father's mistakes, then he is also quite able to help my four sons forgive my mistakes and reach maturity in spite of them!

When our high school graduating class returned home to celebrate our twenty-fifth reunion, I expected that our fellowship would be marked by a spirit of gaiety with lighthearted conversation. Instead, to my surprise our banquet was more like a religious service. There was a spirit of reverence as the class president, now a college professor of languages, called on us to remember the deceased class members. The community center where we met was hallowed that day by a deep sense of gratitude for the gift of life which we all still possessed. Our solemn attitude toward life sprang, it seemed to me, from that fear of dying that is in us all to one degree or another. The fear was there, but faith was there also. As we thought of the death of several class members, and of our own inevitable passing sooner or later, we were able to face the reality of death, refuse to be overwhelmed by the fear of it, and quietly affirm our gratitude for life while it lasts.

This is the victory which faith makes possible no matter what face fear wears. And it is a victory made possible by the saving presence of One who still walks over the waters of our troubles to guide us through our storms. If we will let him, he will speak

to us those calming words he spoke long ago on a
stormy day to his friend Isaiah:

> Fear not, for I am with you,
>   be not dismayed, for I am your God;
> I will strengthen you, I will help you,
>   I will uphold you with my victorious
>   right hand (Isa. 41: 10 RSV).

As you conclude this chapter, close your eyes and
consider where fear is most real in your life.
Acknowledge your fear; give yourself permission to
be afraid and still belong to Christ. Then imagine
Jesus coming to you, accepting you in spite of your
fear, reaching out to place his hands on your
shoulders, and helping you to claim the victory of
faith.

5

The Reassurance We All Need

> But at once Jesus spoke to them.
> "It's all right! It's I myself,
> don't be afraid!" *Matthew 14:27*

These words reveal the great concern Jesus had
for his friends when he realized how terrified they
were. The moment he knew their need, he began to
meet it. His words of reassurance were spoken "at
once." They needed his help. They wanted his help.
Immediately he helped them by calming their fear.

The darkest hour may be faced if we can only
experience the Master's coming to us. I remember
so clearly the first time I ever closed my eyes and
with believing faith pictured Christ walking up to
me, looking into my eyes, speaking to me about my
deepest need. You may say it was only imagination,
but I can assure you that it was one of the most
moving moments in my life.

All my earlier religious training had programed
me to believe that Christ would come striding up
to me, pointing a long, accusing finger at me. There
would be great disappointment in his face, and stern
words of rebuke and condemnation flowing from
his lips. Instead, I saw him walk up to me and stand
quietly. He looked deeply into my eyes. His was

the most understanding, loving face I have ever seen. Then, without a word of criticism, he reached out and put his right hand on my shoulder and gently spoke words which melted my heart: "Walter, you don't have to impress me, because I really love you as you are. So stop trying so hard. Relax, and just be my man."

His words went straight to the heart of my deepest need: the need to accept myself, and his love, and realize that I don't have to work like a Trojan to become acceptable. Several years have passed since he "came to me" with these words, but the reality of it, the truth and power of it, remain lodged in my heart. A hundred times since, I have caught myself on the "try harder" treadmill. Remembering his counsel, I have tried to relax and just be his person.

So as he came to the disciples, he still comes to us, when we look for him, expect him, and receive him. And by encouraging us, he enables us to encourage each other within the church, to offer encouragement to others outside the circle of faith wherever we encounter them.

Consider the powerful benefit of encouragement as we experience it within the church. As a teenager, I was struggling with the call to the ministry. My pastor helped me to sort out my feelings. I do not remember a single sentence he ever spoke to me, but for more than twenty years I have remembered that he believed in me! Whenever I recall Pastor Griffin Lloyd, that fact shines brightly in my memory: he believed in me! He made me feel that I, even I, could be of value to the kingdom of God!

During several months when despair had me at

wits' end, a friend in our church sent me cards for the sole reason of cheering me up. She would write a note saying, "Though these may be difficult days for you, there are those who appreciate you more than you know, and are grateful for all you are trying to do." It was as though she were standing with me. No matter what the message on each card, what came across to me was: "Hang in there and keep your chin up; you can make it!" Who could put a price tag on the encouragement that just one such friend can provide when you are down?

Paul advised the Christians in Corinth to work toward "building up the church" (1 Cor. 14:12 RSV), using prophecy "so that all may learn and all be encouraged" (14:31 RSV). The encouragement of the brethren was an essential function of the body of Christ. We have observed that the early church grew as a result of persecution. But the church apparently also grew as a result of encouragement.

When the church at Jerusalem sent Barnabas to Antioch to help the new converts, the first thing Barnabas did was to encourage the believers. As a result of this good man's encouragement, "a considerable number of people became followers of the Lord" (Acts 11:24). So encouragement is at the heart of both evangelism and edification! When Christians practice encouragement, others are attracted to the faith, to Christ, and to his body.

Often God's loving acceptance is made known to us through the encouragement of a brother. Speaking at a Bible Conference in Pennsylvania, I felt nervous and uncertain that I would be accepted. The resident bishop, John Warman, was also on the program, and I had never met him. After my first address, the first man up to the platform to greet me was in his shirt sleeves, without a coat or tie. Grasping my hand, he said with a warm smile, "We are truly brothers!" Somehow the Lord and the bishop both knew of my need to be encouraged, and together they met my need. How gracious is our Lord to reassure his frightened disciples!

He comes to us; he sends us to others. Think for a moment. What person near you day after day may be hungry for encouragement, someone you can encourage if you try? What face appears in your mind? Someone at work? At home? At school? A troubled attendant at the service station where you often get gas?

A woman said to me, "I don't think I love my mother. In forty years she has never once commended me or praised me for anything I have ever done. I don't believe she really loves me, and I don't think I love her." Had love died in the absence of encouragement? Yes. Does love thrive in the presence of praise and encouragement? Yes! A psychiatrist advised a husband who had marital trouble, "Go home and learn to praise your wife, even if it frightens her at first!"

Encouragement is the soil in which people grow. Cheer, hearten, inspire another, and you are in touch with life, and Christ is life. Follow Christ and often you will be walking across troubled waters to reassure a brother that he can make it. In the process you yourself will be given new strength.

So in the midst of anxious moments, remember to listen for that inner voice which has power to calm the boisterous waves of the soul. His words alone provide the reassurance we all need.

6

Acting on Impulse

"Lord, if it's really you," said Peter,
"tell me to come to you on the water."
Matthew 14:28

For twenty centuries men have claimed that this
passage reveals a basic weakness in Peter's character.
So Peter takes a licking every time we read this
story.

William Barclay does admit that there are "worse
sins" than Peter's trait of impulsiveness. He excuses
Peter on the basis that his "whole trouble was that
he was ruled by his heart." Nevertheless, Barclay
voices the standard criticism when he says: "Peter
was given to acting upon impulse and without thinking of what he was doing. It was his mistake that
again and again he acted without fully facing the
situation and without counting the cost. He was to
do exactly the same when he affirmed undying and
unshakable loyalty to Jesus (Matthew 26:33-35),
and then denied his Lord's name."*

The critics are right, of course, but is there not
another side to every coin? Must we not admit that

* *The Gospel of Matthew*, Volume 2, page 106.

there is some merit in acting on impulse, especially when our action is in response to the Lord himself?

While we do not want to go so far as to praise irrational behavior, is it not true that we must often act on impulse if we are to consistently obey the Holy Spirit? Surely many deeds of love and mercy would be left undone if we never acted impulsively in response to what we believe to be the leadership of the Spirit!

Obedience to his Spirit is not always a matter of cool calculation or a calm, rational response to what we know is the will of God. Sometimes we are not sure about his will. Sometimes we are not sure in what direction he wants us to move. This is where faith comes in. As with Abraham, often we must move out not knowing our destination, discovering only upon arrival that we have made the correct decision.

Allowance for the impulsive deed of faith is even more necessary because of the manner in which the Holy Spirit works in our minds and hearts. His voice is usually more of a whisper than a shout. He does not push or shove us into obedience. Rather, he nudges us. And his is a gentle nudge. Most of us know the disappointing pain of having failed to recognize his gentle nudging, discovering to our sorrow that we missed an opportunity to do his will. The impulse was there; but we resisted it, settling for "rational" behavior rather than daring obedience. So at least one mark of Christian maturity is the development of this capacity to recognize the gentle nudging of his Spirit, so that we may more consistently do his will.

I cannot help but wonder how many blessings might have passed me by had I never acted impulsively in response to what I interpreted as nudgings of his Spirit! My wife and I attended the first Christian Ashram held near Orlando, Florida. There we heard E. Stanley Jones for the first time. I went as a troubled preacher, struggling in my first appointment out of seminary, longing for that sense of assurance that John Wesley found at Aldersgate.

I had the " impulse" to talk privately with Brother Stanley (the title he preferred), but almost dismissed it. After all, I was a preacher; having assurance was supposed to be one of my credentials. I was fearful that admitting my need to Stanley Jones would be embarrassing and painful. But like Peter I threw caution to the wind and acted on impulse, and what a blessing resulted!

Sharing my need with Brother Stanley, I was surprised at his understanding and simple response. Quietly he asked if I believed in the promises of Jesus. Of course I did. Then he said, "Let's claim one of them for your need." He quoted Mark 11:24, the words of Jesus: "Whatever you pray about and ask for, believe that you have received it, and it will be yours." We knelt together and he prayed that God would give me the assurance I wanted; but more than that, he thanked God that I had received it! Now, more than fifteen years later, I can testify that my need was met completely, and his stabilizing assurance continues to fill my heart. But think what I would have missed had I not acted impulsively!

When I was pastor of the Government Street United Methodist Church in downtown Mobile, people frequently walked in off the street and joined our worship services. One Sunday night a woman who was quite drunk came in and sat down on the back pew. This happened shortly after the service had begun. She soon began to make her presence known by asking questions in a loud voice. The congregation froze, no one looking back at her, but most of them smiling or chuckling softly.

Finally one woman, acting I think on impulse, walked back and sat down beside the woman. She spoke quietly to her, put her arm around her, and allowed the poor, dirty, drunken woman to crumple in her arms and cry softly during the remainder of the service. Afterward the impulsive woman learned that our street friend was homeless. A victim of five tragic marriages, she was wandering aimlessly across country. Her name was Gracie.

Gracie's soiled dress smelled like something out of the trash heap, but she was a person in need. The impulsive woman in our church found her a place to sleep, helped her get a bath and some clean clothes, sought to encourage her to hang on, and assisted her with a ride to the home of her relatives. We do not know, but perhaps Gracie has turned around and found herself. This we do know: the woman who acted on impulse, reaching out in love to Gracie, has never regretted her action! Others sat cowering in their pews, resisting perhaps the impulse to help. One woman moved quickly, without thinking. In this she was much like Peter. Perhaps we might call her the Good Samaritan Woman—impulsive, but obedient!

One day a man walked into my study without an appointment. He explained, "I was sitting at home thinking about my problem when it occurred to me that I should come talk with you." We shared together as he confessed sins committed more than twenty years before. "I'm not sure God has forgiven me, and I don't have peace in my heart about all of this," he said. He needed to hear a brother affirm God's forgiveness, and to see in a brother's eyes that he was accepted in spite of his sins. God permitted me to be this brother to him, and as we prayed, a wonderful sense of God's peace came to his soul.

In a moment of time, after twenty years of living in anxiety without God's peace and forgiveness, this man on an impulse came to seek out his pastor and confess his sins. How wonderful were the results of his impulsiveness!

It happened during a camp meeting in Michigan. Some of us built a bonfire after the service one night. Around it we sang and shared until almost midnight. Only a dozen people remained when I got up to go to bed. As I walked away, a man rose quickly and suggested we have prayer before retiring. As we got in a circle around the dying campfire, he asked that we pray for him, asking the Lord to heal him of pain in his stomach.

Acting on impulse, I asked him if he knew why his stomach was hurting. As soon as he began to reply, I knew immediately that my question had been prompted by the Holy Spirit. His twenty-year-old son had turned his back on his family and his Christian upbringing; he was living a rebellious, wayward life with little regard for the feelings of his father. The father was simply brokenhearted, and he knew that the pain in his stomach was caused by his anguish over his son's behavior. As tears flowed freely down the father's face, all of us in the circle prayed for healing—the healing of the broken relationship of this father and his son. Somehow, in that circle of love in an outdoor setting, we knew that God was answering our prayers!

In a way, we had all acted impulsively, but we had moved toward our Lord in faith. Our obedience had made possible a celebration of love that none of us will ever forget!

I was counseling with a young woman who had very little self–esteem. I had encouraged her to accept her own creativity and to learn to express her deep feelings more. She found it hard to do, especially since her husband often made her feel like a doormat! He ridiculed and teased her unmercifully. Slowly she tried to affirm her own worth and to learn to love herself. Over many months she became a new person, and eventually she was able to write me a beautiful letter.

> After so many years of living in my cocoon I've at last found my way outside and stretched forth my wings to become the beautiful butterfly God intended me to be! It hasn't been easy—finding my way through the outer shell I had so carefully built around my "real" self. And it isn't easy being a butterfly. But it is the most important reality of my life now. Thank you for being my friend until I could become a friend to myself!

She probably wrote that letter on impulse, without giving it much thought. But there is no doubt it was a therapeutic exercise in self–expression, enabling her to express her newfound self–esteem. And I was greatly blessed by her impulsive letter of gratitude, for it came on a dreary day when my own self–esteem needed a lift!

So count the cost and think carefully about what you believe to be the will of God for you as a disciple of Christ. But don't be afraid to risk acting on impulse now and then. You may discover with joyful surprise that you are moving in obedience to the gentle nudging of his Spirit!

Meditate for a few minutes on this thought: *What impulse have I resisted lately that may well be his gentle nudging?*

And consider this: Some joys and blessings will belong to you only when you are willing to act on your impulses. As a beatitude we might express it this way:

Blessed are those who are willing to risk being wrong by acting on impulse, for they shall often experience the joy of knowing they have obeyed the quiet nudgings of my Spirit!

7

It's Your Move

"Come on, then," replied Jesus.
Matthew 14:29a

Our son Steve likes to play checkers—especially
with me since he usually wins! Sometimes as I'm
playing with him, my mind wanders off to other
matters, and I forget to concentrate on the game. So
it is not unusual for Steve to startle me with this
irritated comment: "Dad, it's your move!"

Life is much like a checker game. Action and reaction are part of the game. God's move is first; he
moves toward us in creation with the gift of life.
Having received the gift of life, each of us must
respond. Each new day is God's move. With each
new sunrise, God is saying to every man: "Now it's
your move, my child. What will you do with this
day?"

Recognizing man's need for a Savior, God moved
toward the whole human race by sending his Son to
save us from our sins and open up to us the way to
abundant life. Once God had given Jesus to the
world, he had made his ultimate move. The New
Testament explains that it is his plan for each of us
to respond to his move. This idea is touchingly ex-

pressed in the hymn, "How Firm a Foundation." It appears in the line, "What more can He say, than to you He hath said?" What more indeed can he say once he has made his Word become flesh in Jesus!

God does not dictate our response. Since he has given us a free will, we are free to move away from God in rejection or toward God in acceptance and faith. The apostle John describes God's move in the gift of Jesus. Then he records the sad reality of God's move and the response of many: "He came into his own creation, and his own people would not accept him" (John 1:11). Yet he adds the possibility of a positive move, for "wherever men did accept him he gave them the power to become sons of God" (1:12).

I wonder if Jesus expected Peter to ask for the privilege of walking on the water. He could have ridiculed Peter by saying, "Foolish man, you ask for the impossible! You should know by now you have neither the power nor the faith to duplicate my deeds!" His response to Peter could easily have been a "put down," and the other disciples would have thought it well deserved. But true to his nature, Jesus responded with loving understanding, giving the impetuous apostle a chance to try this new experiment whatever his motive.

The response of Jesus is symbolic of our situation in life. Whatever our circumstances, there is always a sense in which Jesus stands beckoning to us saying, "Come on, then." And in his invitation there is the gracious hope that we may exercise daring faith and discover our potential by walking toward him.

Consider right now, where you are, that Jesus may be saying to you, "Come on." Look into his eyes and realize that he is filled with expectation for you. He believes you can actually make the walk you want so much to make. Across the years of our lives, Jesus comes to us again and again, inviting us to "come on," urging us to walk as he walks.

Where in your life is Jesus saying just now, "It's your move"? Using the rest of this page, write down the first thoughts that come to your mind, stating which "move" you feel he is inviting you to make:

He may be saying, "It's your move," concerning the use of your life. Perhaps you have been made aware that your gifts might be better used in another vocation. A friend of mine gave up a job as a clerk and became a nurse. The move required additional training and the transition was not easy. But she told me she "had to do it." She felt it was the will of God for her life. Once this thought came into her mind (God's move), she found no peace until she had responded in obedience and faith (her move). As a nurse she has found joy and satisfaction in her work. A sense of inward peace about the use of her life came to her.

Jesus may be saying, "It's your move," about your sins. You have sins you have not confessed, sins for which you are not sure you have received forgiveness. When you read words like these, you hear God saying that it is your move: "If we freely admit that we have sinned, we find God utterly reliable and straightforward—he forgives our sins and makes us thoroughly clean from all that is evil" (1 John 1:9).

Unconfessed sin can make life miserable. It keeps God's peace out of our hearts, and it may even result in physical and mental illness. The condition of the soul affects the body. A lovely young woman, who always appeared to be happy, came to me one day. In great distress she asked that I pray for God to heal her of a terrible headache. Quietly I felt God's Spirit leading me to ask this question, "Do you know why your head is hurting?"

Her honesty was spontaneous and beautiful. "Yes, I believe I do," she replied. "My head is hurting because I hate my mother. I have hated her for fifteen years, and just the thought of her makes me sick."

Though I was surprised by her answer, I tried to convey understanding and acceptance. Ignoring her headache, I suggested we claim God's promise in 1 John 1:9 and pray for God to forgive her hate and cleanse her heart of all the anger which she had nursed for so many years. Together we believed that she was completely forgiven and that God was indeed cleansing her heart of all hate and hurt.

When we finished praying, her pain was gone. Having confessed her sins to an understanding brother, she had wonderful assurance of God's forgiveness. The next day she reported to me, "I am amazed at how clean I feel! For the first time in my life I feel really clean within, and I have peace with God that I can hardly believe!"

James learned well from Jesus, for he saw the connection between the confession of sin and healing. Remember his beautiful statement: "You should get into the habit of admitting your sins to one another, and praying for one another, so that if sickness comes to you you may be healed" (5:16).

Many times I have heard Jesus saying, "It's your move," with regard to my family. It is so easy for some of us to get caught up in our work and neglect to spend quality time with family members.

One experience stands out in my memory, a time when I learned a good lesson the hard way! One summer our family was participating in a family camp in Michigan. I was one of the speakers. Each afternoon the schedule called for family fun, but I usually became involved in a discussion with adults while our boys played ball. One day Tim, then about eleven, sought me out and tried to persuade me to go canoeing in a nearby stream. As I explained to Tim that I would not be able to go, I heard the Spirit's inner voice saying, "Don't be a fool; go with him!"

So I went! And that afternoon I learned how easy it is to capsize a canoe! It turned out to be one of the happiest occasions our family has ever had together. And I imagine Tim will remember all his life how funny we looked getting baptized again in that unlikely river!

Again and again as I look back on that experience, I have realized that it was "my move" to strengthen family relationships. The need is not always to go "do something" together like canoeing. We must learn the joy of simply being together. As much as anyone, my son Steve has taught me this. Often he will insist on going with me even when no special activity is involved. As I was about to leave home one afternoon to make hospital calls, Steve asked if he could go. "No," I said, pointing out that he was only ten and would not be allowed to visit the patients. But he insisted. "I just want to walk with you. I'll stay in the lobby until you have finished your visits."

I will never forget what Steve said to me as we walked along the sidewalk toward the hospital. He reached out and put his hand in mine, and as we walked along holding hands he said, "Dad, I like to be with you; we have a lot of fun doing things together, don't we?" Joy welled up within me as I smiled back at him!

Stopping along the way to smell the fragrance of the flowers can bring double joy if we have learned how much more fun it is to smell them while holding hands with someone God has given us to love!

We may hear Jesus saying, "It's your move," as we consider our capacity to love other people. Few of us have reached our full potential to really care about others.

My experience with Pop West helped me discover that I still have much to learn about really loving others. Pop was dying with cancer, and he was aware of his condition. He knew he didn't have much time left, for he was past seventy-five and very weak. Visiting him was not easy for me. I liked Pop and it hurt me to see him suffer. Usually his dear wife was with him, and I would read a favorite passage of scripture before we prayed together. It was always a very moving encounter.

As his condition grew worse, it was necessary for Pop's visitors to don a sterile gown and face mask before entering his room. Pop's delightful sense of humor permitted me to joke with him by saying, "Well, Pop, your angel has come back to see you!" Even in pain he would smile and reply that it would take more than a mask and a gown to disguise me as an angel!

After visiting with Pop, I would offer a prayer and leave. But one afternoon, before I began to pray, he asked that I take his hand in mine. So holding the hand of my dying friend, I prayed. When I finished I started to withdraw my hand, but he held my hand securely in his. Then he began to pray himself. And such a prayer I had never heard! It was as though God's Spirit was reaching out to me through Pop.

There was not an ounce of self-pity or concern for himself in his prayer. He was not angry at God for allowing him to suffer. Rather, he was totally con-

cerned for his pastor! He thanked God for sending
me to him, for giving me strength to do my work,
for using me to bless others. As though he were
talking to a close friend he had known for years,
he asked God to fill my heart with his love, to meet
all my needs, and to keep on using me for his glory.
Through this experience with Pop I felt that I had
been lifted near to the heart of God!

Walking down the corridor out of the hospital, I
could not help but tingle with amazement at what
had just happened. A dying man, who had every
reason to be absorbed in his own suffering, had risen
above his own pain long enough to reach out in love
to lift my heart to the throne of grace. Pop was evidently so surrendered to God's Spirit that his Spirit
was able to reach out and touch my spirit with healing love. What a lesson! I brushed tears away as I
realized from Pop's example how little I have learned
about really loving others. How much there is to learn
about caring for others unselfishly!

Where in your own life is the Lord saying just now,
"It's your move"?

8

Courage to Take the First Step

Peter stepped down from the boat
and did walk on the water, making
for Jesus. *Matthew 14:29b*

The usual focus of this story is on poor, faithless
Peter sinking beneath the waves, calling out to Jesus
for help. But take another look. Let this one single
moment in the story sink into your mind. There before unbelieving eyes, ours and the disciples', are
two men walking on the water! John says Peter
walked on the water, too!

Try to put yourself in Peter's sandals. Impulsively
you have asked Jesus to let you walk to him on
the water. Rather than rebuke you for your unusual
request, Jesus invites you to come on. As you raise
one foot over the edge of the boat, suddenly you
realize how foolish you must appear to the other
disciples. You are flushed with the awareness that
their eyes are upon you, wondering if you have lost
your mind!

Then you look down at the water, and the thought
occurs to you: *If I step out there, I'll sink like a
rock, and these guys won't stop laughing for a week!*
So you turn and smile sheepishly at the disciples,
and calling out to Jesus, you say, "That's all right,

Lord. I was only kidding. Come on over to the boat and talk to us awhile."

It takes but little imagination to suppose the story might have turned out that way. But the point is, it did not, even though Peter surely must have had second thoughts about getting out of the boat.

So let's give him credit for the courage it must have required to take that first step. He got out of his boat. He was willing to risk appearing foolish in order to try something new, something he did not know would work. Giving up the security of his boat, he stepped out into the unknown on faith. If he had played it safely, he would never have known whether he could walk on water or not.

Though Peter later began to sink, notice here also the direction in which Peter was moving. He was making for Jesus! Though he was not perfect, he was moving in the right direction—toward his Lord. At the time of Jesus' trial later on, Peter would move in the wrong direction—away from Jesus— out of fear that he might also be crucified as one of his disciples. For this moment now at least he is able to overcome his timidity and fear. He acts on faith.

It is often necessary for us to give up the security of the known and comfortable to realize the potential of the uncertain adventure. The Christian must be prepared to leave the boat of safety to walk toward the Christ who constantly beckons us to walk with him on untried waters. It is only in the exercise of such daring faith that our greatest potential may be realized.

Our family was comfortable in Nashville, Tennessee, where I served as a staff member on the

Board of Evangelism of our denomination. Our work in the lay witness ministry was at an all-time high. I was relatively safe in the boat of success. There seemed no reason to doubt that we could have stayed on in this ministry indefinitely.

But there was a restlessness in our hearts. As my wife Dean and I talked about our lives together, we felt drawn toward a pastoral setting. The tension from my frequent travels was creating serious difficulties in our family relationships. Dean was definite in her feelings. "You need to be in the pastorate, for your sake and the sake of our family," she said one evening in May.

At the time, my reply was rather abrupt. Irritated at her insistence on a change, I replied, "You know that I have not turned down any offers lately to go to a church!" That might have ended the matter, except that less than three hours later a startling phone call came. It was an invitation to take up a challenging pastorate!

My wife and I were both sure God had opened a door for us, but it was not easy to walk through it. The security of our Nashville position was hard to leave. There would be those who would not understand; some would consider us foolish to exchange the privilege of national influence for one local church. Somehow we found the courage to leave Nashville. In return God has given the assurance that we are in his will. We are experiencing fulfillment and joy we would have never known had we stayed in the Nashville boat.

One day a member of our church board walked into my study. He had become rather careless in church attendance. I had never talked to him before though I had been his pastor for six months. Quickly he made his point. "I'm ashamed of myself," he said. "I could give you a lot of excuses, but the truth is, I've just gotten out of the habit of coming to church. I have been busy with a lot of things, but I know I've been letting you down. I want to get back on the right track."

Gazing into his eyes, I was moved almost to tears of joy myself as I saw a big tear trickle down his cheek. I praised God within my heart for the privilege of sharing this moment of "turning" with my brother! Before he left we prayed together, and he walked out of my office with "newness of life" beaming from his eyes.

This experience of new life would not have been possible had not my brother found the courage to take the first step—the step that led to this life-changing encounter with God and his pastor.

A young woman's husband died when she was only thirty, leaving her with three small children. She slowly sank into bitterness and self-pity, becoming neglectful of worship. Wrapped up in herself, she was a neat little package of selfishness. But the members of her prayer group, the one she had once attended faithfully, would not stop caring. They continued to pray for her, to love her, and to encourage her. After many months there came a beautiful moment at the close of a Sunday morning service when she walked down the aisle. Grasping my hand firmly, she said, "God has brought me through a long night, but thank God I am through it. Now I want you to give me something to do to help others."

She had fought her way out of her own cocoon, and she had decided to climb out of the boat of self-pity. The aisle of that church was water on which she was walking toward Christ! It took genuine courage for her to take the first step.

A man volunteered to drive me to the airport in Orlando after I finished a speaking engagement at a layman's retreat. As we cruised down the highway, I noticed that the speedometer was registering almost eighty miles per hour. I was nervous but decided not to criticize my benefactor.

He began to share an unusual experience he'd had that morning at the retreat. He had gone into the small prayer room to pray; after a brief period of intercessory prayer, he arose from his knees to leave. He was startled as he looked at the simple altar. When he had knelt to pray, two candles beside the cross were burning. When he opened his eyes to leave, one of the candles had gone out!

That in itself did not seem unusual to me, until he went on to tell me that he was seventy-five and had already suffered three serious heart attacks. "Do you suppose," he said, his voice trembling, "that was God's way of telling me my life was soon to be snuffed out like that candle?"

The way he was driving I was really afraid he was going to snuff out my candle and his own, too, at any minute!

He persisted in asking me to help interpret his experience. "How would you respond to it?" he asked. I suggested that he try not to be alarmed by it, but go home, sit down, and take a long, serious look at his priorities. "Sort them out as best you know how, and then ask the Lord to help you live one day

at a time, celebrating each day as a gift from God,"
I advised him.

Weeks later I heard from him. He wrote that he
was still alive, doing his best to live each new day
in an attitude of celebration and gratitude. For him
faith requires courage to take the first step each
day. He walks over the restless waters of ill health,
not knowing which day will be his last.

All of us face different circumstances, but each
of us struggles with the temptation to stay in the
comfortable safety of his present situation. It is
never easy to step over the side of the boat into the
waters of the new challenge. Yet we must take the
risk if our full potential in discipleship is to be realized.

Imagine for a moment that Jesus is speaking to
you in your present circumstances. You are in your
boat of safety, satisfied with your situation. Able to
manage things quite well on your own, you don't
need much help. But Jesus beckons you to get out
of your boat and walk toward him in faith.

If you get out of your boat, and move toward him,
what risk will you have to take? What is it that you
must do? What water must you walk over if you
accept his invitation?

Take your pen and write down what comes to
mind. Do it quickly. Write down exactly what you
must do to get both feet out of your boat and on
the unknown water of Christ's new adventure for
you.

9

Handling Failure

But when he saw the fury of the wind
he panicked and began to sink. . . .
Matthew 14:30a

In athletics we are prone to think that "winning is everything." So in our culture losing is often traumatic. Success is such a god among us that most of us don't know how to lose or accept failure.

A recent heavyweight champion boxer spent thousands of dollars on disguises so that whenever he lost a fight, he could leave the dressing room without being recognized. Most of us who have experienced failure can understand how he felt.

Yet life demands that we learn how to handle failure or we will sink ourselves in the sea of despair. The question is not whether we fail but how shall we handle the inevitable failings that come to us all. No matter how often we are flushed with the thrill of victory, eventually each of us stands with his head bowed, lamenting with the psalmist:

I am slipping down the hill to death; I am shaken off from life as easily as a man brushes a grasshopper from his arm. My knees are weak from fasting and I am skin and bones. I am a symbol of failure to all mankind; when they see me they shake their heads (Ps. 109:22-25, THE LIVING BIBLE).

Rare indeed is the man who does not at some time in his life feel like that grasshopper.

For many years "despair" was more a word than an experience to me. It was something other people experienced and Norman Vincent Peale wrote about. As a young man I was able to manage life and achieve most of my goals without much thought of failure. My classmates described my cocky attitude with this line that appeared under my picture in our high school annual:

> "Ah, he's some fellow I'm telling you;
> There's not a thing that he can't do."

But the years of smooth sailing ended abruptly when the doctor advised us that our son was dying with leukemia. Suddenly I saw what Peter saw—the fury of the vicious winds that beat and threaten us on life's sea. As our prayers failed to still the cruel winds of suffering and death, we found ourselves humbled by circumstances we could not manage.

Mercifully God did not leave us alone in the ashes of our heartache. He came to us, and only then did we begin to learn the meaning of grace and faith. Gently God led us away from the fountain of bitterness, self–pity, and anger. Slowly we found that in our misery he was teaching us and molding character out of chaos. Years beyond our loss now, we can see that losing a loved one can deepen one's understanding of others, produce godly sympathy, and increase one's capacity to identify with others in their trouble.

I saw the grace of God at work in my wife more

than in myself in those days when we were trying
to handle the tragedy of our son's death. She reached
out to God for understanding and he gave it. Without any training for poetic expression, she still felt
compelled to share poetically the creative insights
that came in our darkness. My favorite is "The Children's Wing," for I remember vividly how much
pain we saw in the children's wing of the Baptist
Hospital in Nashville during those bleak winter days.
But somehow Dean saw beyond the pain a loving
Father working for our good.

The Children's Wing

There is a place all set apart,
Where only children stay.
A place where nurses dart
About their work both night and day.

And when you look about,
You see most everything,
From Danny who is burned,
    To Steve who passes out,
In this place called the Children's Wing.

It takes a strong heart and faith
To witness all the pain;
Yet you know God abideth
Here in the Children's Wing.

On each little bed a child doth lay,
One with curly locks, another a pony tail.
You look at each one not knowing what to say,
So you pray to God your smile will not fail.

Here you see true love expressed
By mothers or fathers who care;
While some don't know they're blessed
And think their burdens too much to bear.

Here is a place to count your blessings,
When you hear the little children sing.
You can thank God for the testings
That come here in the Children's Wing.

Dean's attitude reveals one of the great secrets of handling failure: to see God at work in the midst of it and hold on to Him in spite of the pain. Such faith enables a man at the end of his rope to tie a knot in it and hold on!

My own faith in the goodness of God was strengthened by the reality of grace at work in Dean. To see God at work in one's companion seems to verify the witness of the Scriptures, so that one can more readily believe the faith that Paul demonstrated many times. One scene especially comes to mind when I think of Paul's testings—that time in the city of Lystra when a murderous mob stoned him and dragged him out of the city, and left him for dead. But miraculously a small group of believers gathered around Paul until, as Luke tells it, "he got up and went back into the city" (Acts 14:20)!

Think of it: his mission here ended in failure, and he was near death. Yet he went right back into the city to start all over again! His faith was not shaken; his attitude was not in the least pessimistic. You might expect that he would return to Lystra to wail and whine how badly he had been treated by the Jews. Instead, he and Barnabas were able to help the believers to "grow in love for God and each other." Paul rose from failure and encouraged others! No wonder the church grew in strength as God blessed the witness of this courageous man! He kept tying knots in the end of his rope!

And Peter tied some knots of his own, too. Failing in his attempt to walk on the water to Jesus was not the last failure for this big fisherman. Again and again he would fall on his face until finally his failure was matched only by the betrayal of Judas. After the cruel crucifixion of Jesus, Peter must have felt smaller than an ant as the reality of his own cowardice settled like a pall over him. John pictures Peter as discouraged, returning to his fishing boat to ponder his brief journey with Jesus.

Then the resurrected Jesus appears on the beach, inviting Peter and his friends to join him for breakfast. Surely Peter approached Jesus cautiously, fearful that he would be castigated for his lying and ridiculed in front of the other fishermen. But the tender, compassionate Christ talked to Peter not of sin but of love, and the opportunity to feed his sheep. What a lesson on how to handle failure this must have been for Peter!

Jesus was never one for dodging reality. But here we see his refusal to focus on a man's weaknesses. Rather, he appeals to the best in Peter and challenges him to take up a life of love. And that is just what Peter did. The attitude Jesus had toward him—accepting, forgiving, understanding—was all he needed to recover from his failure and get back on the right track.

So it is with us. In the midst of our failures we should remember that our Lord understands; as we look to him we also find strength to bounce back. And all around us are our brothers and sisters, often sinking in the boisterous waves of defeat. They are desperate for even one person who will look into their eyes with understanding love. Observe then with joy the glory of this faith walk with Christ. In spite of our weakness he comes to us to help us handle our failures, and the help we receive enables us better to assist our brothers!

10

The Right Source of Help

> . . . calling out, "Lord save me!"
> *Matthew 14:30b*

Apparently Peter had been so impressed by the Master's power to walk on the water that he momentarily forgot about the storm. But as soon as he left the boat to try this miraculous feat himself, he remembered the angry waves. Matthew suggests that it was only after Peter turned his eyes away from Jesus and looked at the turbulent waves, that he began to fear, and to sink.

Notice the sequence of events in this passage as described in the New English Bible: "But when he saw the strength of the gale he was seized with fear; and beginning to sink, he cried, 'Save me, Lord.'" As long as he kept his eyes on Jesus, he was able to walk on the water. But as soon as he looked away from Jesus, giving all his attention to his predicament, he became afraid and began to fail. When his focus changed from his Lord to his trouble, first fear, then failure, came swiftly. There is a lesson here. Whenever we are more impressed with our problems than we are with the power of Christ, we are likely to be overwhelmed by our problems.

But perhaps there is an even more significant lesson here. Observe that it was to his Lord, and not to his friends, that Peter immediately turned for help. So while we may chastise him for turning his eyes away from Jesus, we must give him credit for this: when fear seized him, he turned to the right source for help!

Peter might have turned just as easily to Andrew back in the security of the boat and said, "Throw me a rope, brother!" It would have been a natural reaction to turn back to the familiar and the comfortable, rather than risk getting further away from the boat. He knew the boat would float, but walking on water was quite a new adventure in faith! So it is a mark of courage that, having made his move toward Jesus, Peter did not turn back when he panicked. He may have recalled what Jesus said one day to a hesitant follower: "Anyone who puts his hand to the plow and then looks behind him is useless for the kingdom of God" (Luke 9:62).

Much human misery results from men's seeking help in the wrong places. All of us have the need to be significant. But often we seek significance in ways either destructive or unproductive. A man wanting to succeed in his work may begin drinking alcoholic beverages because "in my business it is necessary." His goal is significance in his vocation, but in the end he may destroy himself and others. He needs help but goes to the wrong source.

A little six-year-old girl in an Advent candlelighting service had the special assignment of lighting the first Advent candle. She had been instructed to touch the taper of the candlelighter to the wick of the candle. But no one thought to tell her that first she must light the taper from one of the candles burning on the altar. When her turn came, she carefully raised the candlelighter and touched the taper to the wick of the candle she was supposed to light. Naturally nothing happened! She had not gone to the source of fire, so her unlighted taper was helpless! Eventually a wise mother helped her light the taper, and she completed her mission.

Is this not a picture of many people, going through the motions of life correctly but with unlighted tapers? They want the right results, but they have never gone to the Source of divine fire for the help they need!

Pride is the ugly demon that keeps us away from the Source. We don't want to admit we need God's light, so we call our darkness light and pretend we have all the fire we need. Yet the help we need is very near. The lighted candle the little girl needed was only three feet away, but it could not light her taper until she admitted her need for the candle's help!

Returning from a journey to Michigan, our family was stranded for several hours with car trouble. It happened one Saturday night on an interstate highway far away from any large city. I sought help at the nearest service station, but found none. The attendant wanted to help me but could think of no way to assist me until Monday. He suggested we spend the night and all day Sunday in a nearby motel and get the car fixed Monday. But some way or other I had to get home and be in my pulpit the next morning.

About ten o'clock that night, I remembered that my dad lived about fifty miles away; perhaps he could help. But because of my pride I was reluctant to call him. My wife would probably say, "Oh, sure, call your daddy; you're past forty and still have to call your daddy to bail you out of trouble!" The prospect of appearing unable to manage things without daddy's help caused me to hesitate.

Finally, in desperation, I called him and asked if he knew where I might obtain a starter for our car at that time of night. He thought for a moment, then replied, "Yes, I think so; I'll see if I can get it for you and have your brother drive it down to you." By midnight my brother Seth had arrived with the starter, and within an hour we were on our way home. As we journeyed along the highway home, the family exhausted and asleep, a beautiful thought suddenly occurred to me. It was so beautiful that it moved me to tears. I could hardly see the highway.

I had been unable to help myself, but pride kept me from turning immediately to my father. Finally I had swallowed my pride and called my father, and he had sent his son to my rescue! Those words leaped up in my heart like heavenly music: I called my father and he sent his son! What I had experienced was the very essence of the gospel! Man in his sin cannot save himself, but God has provided for his salvation. Yet pride keeps a man from admitting his need of the Father's help. And it is only when a man acknowledges his need that the Father is able to send his Son to rescue man from his sins.

The help I needed had been available all during those hours of worry, when I had been looking to other sources for help. So it is with many people who need help but are unwilling to turn to God as their source. Emerson's words paint a terrible picture of the predicament of many proud people who stead-fastly refuse to yield to God: "Some men live on the brink of mysteries into which they never enter; and with their hand on the doorlatch, they die outside."

There is the mystery of the new birth into which many people never enter though they may go to church all their lives. They live on the brink of new-ness of life but never experience it because they are unwilling to make a full surrender to God. Every Christmas they go to church and sing,

> O holy Child of Bethlehem,
> Descend to us, we pray;
> Cast out our sin and enter in,
> Be born in us today.
> —*Phillips Brooks*

But still they never really experience in themselves the birth of the Savior. Conversion remains a mys-tery, and though they may have a hand on the doorlatch, they live and die without personally dis-covering its meaning. So the words of an unknown poet bring a degree of sadness as we reflect on their truth:

> Though Christ a thousand times
> In Bethlehem be born;
> If He's not born in thee
> Thy soul is still forlorn.

One of my favorite stories concerns a man who had my problem of possessing so much pride he was reluctant to turn to his Father for help. It seems this man stumbled over a cliff one night and fell a considerable distance before catching himself on a bush. Looking down, he realized he might be killed if he dropped to the ground, and there seemed to be no way to climb back up. So he began yelling for help. As soon as he yelled out, "Is anybody up there?" a calm voice answered, "Yes, I am here."

He paused in surprise, then replied, "Can you help me?" The voice answered, "Yes, I can help you."

He paused again, then asked, "Who are you?" The voice responded, "I am God."

After another long pause, he asked, "What do you want me to do?" And God answered, "Let go of your limb, and depend on me to save you."

This time there was a long pause. Finally the man called out again, "Is there anybody *else* up there?"

He was unwilling to give up the security of his limb for the uncertain help God was offering. And like so many of us, he was looking for some way to avoid doing business with God—on his terms!

When Peter realized he needed help, he went to Jesus, the right source, for help. There was faith in his plea, "Save me!" He did not say, "If you can, save me." He knew that Jesus could help him, and he did.

When we follow Peter's example, we discover what Peter did: Jesus is the right source of help, and his help is near and available!

11

Love That Never Gives Up

At once Jesus reached out his hand and caught him,
saying, "You little–faith! What made you lose your
nerve like that?" *Matthew 14:31*

Clearly Jesus was disappointed in Peter. He had
spent many hours praying for Peter. For many
months he had worked patiently with Peter and his
other disciples, instructing them in the meaning of
faith. Over and over it had pained our Lord to observe what little faith his followers had, in spite of
much teaching and many miracles. Now in this crisis
he wanted so much for Peter to rise to the occasion
and exercise mature faith. But not so. Doubt finally
prevailed, and an embarrassed Peter began to slip
beneath the waves.

Knowing how we might have reacted to Peter, we
would not have been surprised had Jesus reacted dif-
ferently. Jesus might well have cried out in disgust,
"Throw the poor fellow a rope, boys, and pull him
back in! What a disgusting demonstration of faith!
He should have stayed in the boat!"

Jesus could have concentrated on Peter's failure,
heaping ridicule upon him and inviting the other
disciples to laugh at Peter's pathetic, waterlogged
example. With a little encouragement the fellows in

the boat could have had a laugh at Peter's expense.

Observe, however, that there is little ridicule, scorn, or criticism in our Lord's attitude. Instead, the text reveals something priceless and beautiful about Jesus: he did not hesitate to come to Peter's aid when the disciple cried for help! Jesus did not have to reflect on the matter; every translation of this scene shows that Jesus reached out *immediately* to help Peter. Our Lord's help was available *at once!*

Here is another window into the heart of God. Man's failure does not weaken God's love for him! God's affection for man remains constant in spite of his sins and weaknesses, for he loves him unconditionally. We often love others on a conditional basis. Ours frequently is an "if" love. *If* your behavior meets with my approval, then I will love you! *If* you disappoint me, then I will stop loving you! God loves us "anyhow." So the Father's love is "anyhow" love. Regardless of our behavior he continues to love us!

Consider the tremendous *lift* Peter must have felt at the response of Jesus. It was more than a lift out of the water. It was a lift in self-esteem. To know that Jesus cared that much about him in spite of his doubt must have boosted Peter's spirit greatly. Surely Peter was tempted to give up on himself, simply to stop trying and throw in the towel. The songwriter caught sight of this "lifting" power of Jesus when he penned the gospel song, "Love Lifted Me." This was exactly what Peter experienced—a love that would not give up on him, but instead lifted him up to a new sense of self-worth!

This was not the only time Peter saw this kind of lifting love in the eyes of Jesus. Every time he fell

on his face, every time he wanted to give up on this
journey in faith, he looked up at Jesus half expecting
that Jesus would be done with him. But it never did
happen! Always when he looked into the face of
Jesus, he saw a love that simply would not give up!
So through every failure, every disappointment,
Christ's love remained like a magnet, drawing him on
toward the will of God! The love which reached out
to Peter that day in the storm was the same love of
which George Matheson wrote so beautifully out of
his blindness:

> O Love that wilt not let me go,
>   I rest my weary soul in thee;
> I give thee back the life I owe,
>   That in thine ocean depths its flow
> May richer, fuller be.

In Christ Peter found a love that would not quit
on him, and so may we, and every seeking soul. The
heart of the gospel is captured in Paul's picture of
this lifting love:

Yet the proof of God's amazing love is this: that it
was *while we were sinners* that Christ died for us
(Rom. 5:8).

God's love is not measured out to us on the basis of
our performance, but it is offered freely no matter
how well or how poorly we perform in the business
of life.

It is this undeserved quality of his love that is so
"amazing" to us. That God can and does love us in
spite of our failures seems to lift us up from defeat

and give us worth and significance as persons. Often we are able to "make it" only because in our hearts there is the "blessed assurance" of his "anyhow" love, and that love lifts us up to climb toward new heights!

Usually we discover the truth of God's love in the loving acceptance of a person, someone who has found peace in his own "acceptedness" and has become free to accept others in the name of Christ. Herein is part of the glory of life. Each of us can not only experience God's undeserved love for ourselves, we can also demonstrate that same kind of love for others. Pascal wisely pointed out that it is man's capacity to *think* that makes him greater even than the universe in which he lives. But thinking is not enough; it is only when a man moves beyond thinking to *loving* that he becomes fully human. And of course we mean *loving* after the manner of Christ, *loving* in the sense of desiring the best for the one we love. Merely to love in the erotic sense, with the focus on our own satisfaction, may prove our humanness, but it does not show forth the dignity possible when life is lived under the Lordship of Christ.

It is just this capacity to love others in a Christlike way that excites me about being a human being. All along the years of our lives we stumble and fall, failing to live up to our best intentions. But as long as we have breath, it remains possible for us to practice "anyhow" love through the indwelling Spirit of Christ! In this, too, we will often fail, but to succeed even occasionally to lift another with our love is to experience the deepest meaning of existence.

I do not intend ever to forget the face of a little boy I met in Mobile one summer. He was one of the

Sunshine Singers, a group of mentally retarded boys and girls who gave a concert in our church. The group arrived at the church while I was out visiting. When I entered the fellowship hall, a young man walked over to me and looked up into my face. With a broad smile he asked, "You want to know my name?"

"Why, I sure do," I replied. "What is your name?"

Still grinning from ear to ear, he said simply, "Me Jeff."

He was obviously proud to be Jeff! Despite his handicap, he glowed with a captivating sense of self-worth. I learned from the chaplain of his school that Jeff was nine years old, and that he had never spoken a word before he was brought to the school at age seven. The chaplain's wife had worked tirelessly with Jeff, teaching him not only how to speak but to sing as well.

That night as the Sunshine Singers sang, I wept quietly as wave after wave of pure joy swept over my soul. At one point in the performance, my friend Jeff stood up on a chair in the midst of the group and sang with gusto one verse of "God Bless America." Standing behind him, not singing herself but holding Jeff about the waist so he would not fall, was the chaplain's wife. As I looked at the two of them, it seemed that a light from heaven penetrated the ceiling of the church so that the faces of the woman and the boy literally shone with the glory of God! I knew that what I had seen was the essence of life at its best—one person helping another person to experience joy and significance!

I knew that I could hardly imagine how difficult

and frustrating had been this woman's task of leading Jeff slowly out of his silence into speech and song. Surely she had been disappointed in Jeff's progress a hundred times. Often she must have wanted to give up on him. No doubt Jeff, who in his early years was not acquainted with such love, had often despaired, losing hope that he could ever speak as others spoke. But whenever he felt like quitting, he would look into the eyes of his teacher, and there he saw a love that refused to give up on him! Thus he was drawn into newness of life!

Our world is filled with people who are struggling to find significance. Tension and trouble threaten to overcome them, and they look desperately for even one person who will keep on believing in them despite their failures. It humbles me to realize that in the midst of my failures God has always sent someone who believed in me with a love that would not give up. And it thrills me to remember that I can be such a person to others in their distress!

My own marriage is knit together today with such a love. Often when I did not deserve her faithfulness, my wife kept on believing in me. When others gave up on me, she did not. Her attitude is best revealed in a spontaneous prayer which she prayed for me one day. I had shared with her my fear and lack of self-confidence about a difficult assignment I was facing. She spoke to the Lord simply and powerfully: "O Lord, help Walter to realize that your power to use him is not limited by his wisdom or knowledge. Give him the assurance of your love and use him for your glory as he offers his best to you. In Jesus' name, Amen." What a lift her love gave me that day!

Despite his failure, Peter was lifted by the love of Jesus, a love that was immediately available when he asked for it.

12

The One Great Lesson

> Then, when they were both aboard the boat, the
> wind dropped. The whole crew came and kneeled
> down before Jesus, crying, "You are indeed the Son
> of God!" *Matthew 14:32, 33*

Some may prefer to believe that Matthew's ac-
count of Jesus walking on the water is really an
allegory rather than an historical event. In discussing
these two possible interpretations, William Barclay
comes to this beautiful conclusion:

> It does not really matter how we take this inci-
> dent; it is in any event far more than the story of
> what Jesus once did in a storm in far–off Palestine;
> it is the sign and symbol of what he always does for
> his people, when the wind is contrary and we are in
> danger of being overwhelmed by the storms of life.*

That indeed is one great lesson of this passage.
And there are other lessons to be gleaned here. Consider, for example, the consequences of this miracle.
Once Jesus and Peter had climbed aboard the boat,
the focus of the disciples shifted from the miracle
itself to the true identity of our Lord. They were
more concerned with *who Jesus was* than with *what*

* *The Gospel of Matthew*, Volume 2, page 106.

he had done. At last the truth was dawning on them: this Nazarene was really the Son of God, the Messiah! Realizing this, they fell down before him in reverence. In a matter of minutes they had moved from fear to worship!

This is the first time in Matthew's Gospel (and in the Synoptics) when the disciples seem really aware that Jesus is the Son of God. They had heard him speak of himself as the Son of God, but they had never with their own lips declared him to be so until this storm subsided. What they had heard now they believed!

Earlier Matthew described another time when Jesus had quieted a storm (chapter 8:23–27). It is interesting to see that on this occasion Jesus was in the boat with the disciples from the beginning and calmed the sea when they cried for his help. But at this time they were only astonished at the power of Jesus. They thought it marvelous that the winds and the waves obeyed his will, but they did not yet understand *why* he possessed that power. Slowly now they are discovering that their Teacher is more than a man, that indeed he is the Savior of the world!

Observe further in this earlier episode that Jesus not only got into the boat, but that the disciples *received* him into the boat. It is easy to imagine their relief to discover that Jesus had come to them. They must have been eager to receive him.

Perhaps on this later occasion they almost capsized the boat as they all got on one side. As Jesus approached with Peter, they were reaching out to help them climb in. They must have remembered that time months before when the winds obeyed his voice!

How important it is for us to realize that we cannot sail the seas of life successfully unless Jesus is in our boat! And that he climbs aboard only by invitation! He does not barge in to take control unless we invite him and receive him. The disciples welcomed him aboard and began to worship him. We must follow their example if we would have the gift of his Presence in the storms of our lives.

But perhaps the great lesson of this experience is that we must learn to *trust Jesus* whether our need is to get out of the boat or to receive Jesus into the boat. In the boat, or out of the boat, trusting Jesus is essential.

No sea is always calm. There are storms for each of us to face. But we need not face a single storm without his Presence—if we can but learn to trust him! To trust him in the dark hours of trials and temptations is never easy.

A friend of mine was cruelly murdered by two thieves. They held him down in a ditch and shot him in the head. At his funeral a young man in the family expressed the struggle in his soul by asking me, "What was God doing when this man was being murdered?"

After a moment of stunned silence, I replied, "I think God was doing the same thing he was doing the day his own Son was murdered—enduring great heartache but working behind the scenes for the redemption of everyone involved, even the killers."

Sometimes God's purposes are made known in the world through a broken heart. It was not easy for the family of my friend to trust Jesus in their hour of sorrow, but it was still the best way for them to get through the storm.

My wife's father died when she was only seven, so she grew up in a home without a father and was often afraid at night. Sometimes she and her oldest sister would sleep in the same bed with their mother, an old shotgun standing beside the bed. My wife remembers that she was so afraid that she would always try to sleep in the middle, between her mother and her sister. She was afraid to sleep on the edge of the bed.

As she grew up she accepted Christ as Lord, and over the years she discovered that while her earthly father was not available to her, she did have a heavenly Father to whom she could turn. She grew in faith and learned that she was loved by her Father. Her Father's love slowly filled her heart and dislodged the fear that had bothered her so many years.

She has learned to trust her Father, so today she is able to sleep without fear on the edge of the bed. Jesus came to her in her storm of childhood fear. As she learned to trust him, he stilled the winds that distressed her. What life–changing power is available to those who trust him!

To learn a great lesson is one thing. But perhaps it is never really learned until you share it with someone else along the way. Surely God teaches us not merely for our own enlightenment, but that we may in turn teach others. To share the joys and insights of the faith journey with others is but to increase the joy we have already received. The Christian walk is no isolated walk, but a journey of sharing and companionship. As every new truth is discovered, we find that we are not alone but linked arm in arm with others like us who are finding joy in similar discoveries. The storms are more bearable because there are others in them with us. Their courage awakens courage in us.

Peter dared to walk out on the water. But suppose he had remembered his brother Andrew, how Andrew had first found Christ, then brought Peter to meet him. Suppose Peter had turned to Andrew before he climbed out of the boat, saying, "Come, brother, let us try this together!"

This at least is the spirit in which we must risk getting out of the boat to trust Jesus—to realize that whatever he teaches us, he means for us to share with others who are struggling in similar storms.

Look carefully about you. Examine every relationship. There is likely one who is waiting, hoping that you will say, "Come, brother, let us walk this way together!"

And as you walk the faith journey together, you will discover that the two of you have been joined by another Companion, even our Lord, for in the storms of life he always comes to those who need him!